The Wit & Wisdom & Recipes of the Financial Coach

By

David Alan Kossak, CEP
The Financial Coach of the First Coast

"Never ever trust a skinny chef"
-DAK

Table of Contents

Disclaimer

This is very important; so please READ IT. I am Jewish, a stereotypical looking Jewish man. I am fat, a stereotypical looking fat man. I am and have been ridiculed (usually by me), the majority of my life. I am telling you now. I love everybody. I just like to make and be made fun of. Much as in the barber shop scene in the great movie, Gran Torino; starring Clint Eastwood of spaghetti western fame, did I mention I love noodles and pasta. I also loved the Vietnamese food scenes in the above mention movie. IF YOU STILL BUY THIS BOOK, YOU HAVE BEEN WARNED, AND I AM NOT RESPONSIBLE FOR YOUR TEARS! Life is hard, and you are dead for a long time, enjoy.....

DAK

Acknowledgments

I want to thank my son Brandon and my sister Karen who had to endure the multiple meals and tastings each time I cooked the recipes in this book. It may sound like fun, but a person can only eat so much and distinguish between the taste and spices for so long. I also want to thank the many people who I have never met; I tried their recipes and made them my own by changing and personalizing them. That means I cooked every one of the recipes in this book. It was and will continue to be a labor of love.

Dedication

This book is dedicated to my mother and father. They taught me the importance of the family meal, good food and most of all to clean my plate after every meal because there are many people who would trade places with me; who are hungry right now. I was forced to cleaned my plate after every meal, I am now fat, or as my mother would say, “Healthy”. My cardiologist says, “Try not to die during this stress test.” I say, “You can’t trust a skinny chef.”

.

Foreword

Eating is very important to me. I love eating. I know there are some people who eat for need. I eat for enjoyment. I used to think, that people who eat very healthy will live longer and have more of a quality of life. I simply don't know if that is true. Quality can be defined in many ways. I define my quality by the enjoyment that I get from a family meal. My goal and hope is that this book will serve as reminder that you can be frugal and still eat well. Lastly, the family meal is a lost tradition, that needs to be brought back, just as an endanger species. I am convince, that the family meal is just as or more important than youth soccer, baseball, football, basketball or gymnastics. If I am wrong you can always go back to the youth leagues

After reading my bio, you might ask yourself, "What does a person who has been in the financial service industry for 35 years, know about cooking?" That would be a very fair question. The answer will be up to you to determine. The only way to determine whether I know what I'm talking about is by buying this book. That is called wealth accumulation; one thing that cannot be questioned is my knowledge of the financial service industry. You bought the book, I made the royalty. Back to, "What does a person who has been in the financial service industry for 35 years, know about cooking?" All you have to do is prepare the recipes and then allow your family to decide whether the meal was good or bad. I'm betting on good.

Unlike other cookbooks I will not be focusing on the nutritional aspect of each meal, remember, I am fat ("*healthy*")! However, I have been told that many recipes that I have enclosed in fact are quite healthy, who would have thunked it! I am waiting to hear from Dr. OZ. Isn't he great; I love how he makes the guest from his studio audience who are height deprived like me, feel so good about themselves; as opposed to the Biggest Loser television show? I would pay to see a reunion show for ALL past winners. I bet they would need a wide angle television lens to get all of the past winners on the small screen; in this case one would have own a HD 75 inch wall model. I digress.

I do care about taste, quantity and cost. I believe you can feed a family of 4 four for under $200.00 a week, if you use what is available to you, and if you shop "*smart*". Let me restate the goal; 3 meals a day, 7 days a week or 21 meals a week per person. There are four in our family, which means there are 84 meals a week, I must be crazy! Well, I guess there is always the financial service industry to fall back on.

The only way to accomplish this feat is to make informed decisions. An example, purchase spices made from a lesser known company. The savings can be as much as 50 to 100 percent from the spices of a more well-known company.

It means spending as little as 30 minutes one day a week; usually Sundays looking for coupons. One key item you need to keep in mind: you need to purchase store brands as opposed to name brands. Truthfully, there is little to no difference between the two. If you don't believe me look at the nutrition labels on each product.

One thing is for sure, my way is less expensive than going out to fast food chains, spending more and getting less, and certainly my way is a lot healthier. There is one more benefit, your family. Getting to know each other again, having a conversation, getting involved in your children's lives. Family meals were one of my favorite times growing up, the companionship was the best, though my mother was "challenged"; she did not know the difference between a oven, crock pot, or microwave or how they should be used

I promise that you will not be eating hot oatmeal or cold cereal for breakfast. Nor will you be stuck eating weeds with oil, vinegar and lemon wedges for lunch. Your family's dinners will no longer be boring. They will be fun, valuable, and for the most part, easy and fast. To top it off, your family dinners will be tasty and plentiful. The rest of the world makes fun of our portions, they are probably right. Let's face it America was always known for bigger and better. What I am trying to say is that these meals will be American sized.

I still picture the family scene in Norman Rockwell's painting, Freedom from Want, illustrating the family eating together over a meal. Unfortunately, those days are now gone, but they don't have to be, you do have a choice. We go to fast food restaurants, eat in our cars, on the way to soccer, ballet, football, baseball, karate, or worse yet, all of them! Trivia point, did you know the Rockwell painting was used as a means to spread war propaganda during WW II. Sell more bonds, actually not bad advice for those older individuals who are risk adverse.

If you still feel after trying out the recipes, including the financial tips which appear throughout this book, that you were cheated—you can return your book to the publisher, however, you will not receive a refund. I will resell your book as *used* on Amazon.com, but I promise to give you a great deal on a buy-back. Remember, my background is financial services. Have you ever noticed that your stock broker has a nice car, nice home, nice boat, and you have nothing?

David Alan Kossak, CEP
Host Managing Money Matters Radio show
The Financial Coach of the First coast
Aspiring Chef

PS. I don't buy or sell stocks!

Chapter One
"The Invasion of the Coupon Snatchers"

They have invaded our stores, even our neighborhoods. We have even seen these *"coupon people"* on day time TV. I also thought the majority of this breed of individuals cut coupons because they had no life. So I thought!

They spend their time going from website to website, printing off coupons or sending them to their phones or tablets. They steal coupons on products still on the shelves, so the actual buyer of the product receives nothing. Their websites have cute names, like *Coupon Suzy* or *Snip & Snap*. They are designed to get the rest of us to join their species. I suspect before long, coupon people will have their own dating web site. We've all heard of Match.com, so why not Couponcupid.com? I can see their company slogan now, "Where love means never having to pay retail." Wow! That last statement needs to be trademarked. Sometimes I have a moment of clarity and genius.

There are also the traditionalists (myself included), who wait anxiously for the Sunday paper to arrive at our doorstep so that we can pull out our old rusty pair of scissors and start clipping. We are on the fence, half normal shopper, half coupon person.

My children saw me using this cutting device and immediately were dumb struck by the barbaric appliance known as scissors—which was similar to when they saw an iron. My offspring informed me to go directly to the product's manufacture's website where you could simply download the coupons and not get newspaper ink on your hands. "Part of the fun *is* getting the ink on your hands!" I exclaimed.

It was at the heat of the moment when I realized while in conversation with my kids, I had cut the bar code on the coupon in half. Before I could even mourn the loss of my coupon's $. 55 value; I heard a knock on the door and knew immediately I was about to be invaded by the "coupon snatchers". Worse than even the invasion itself, was the fact that the coupon was now not worth the paper it was printed on. I felt a sense of loss as I no longer would be able to save $.55 on *Hebrew National Hotdogs.*

It was happening I was transforming into a new identity. I started to feel a calm come over me, as I began to admire these coupon cutters. I realized I had completely under estimated them and simply did not understand their sense of priority. It was then the transformation was complete, these individuals formerly known as coupon cutters were now known as Coupon Warriors.

One of the things that always amazed me about "coupon warriors" is their organizational ability. I am surprise they don't have their own political party. Like most of our elected officials they have no shame. I mean the average American on food stamps would rather pay full price than reduce their out of pocket cost so they could actually provide more food for their family, than being called a coupon warrior! It would also mean they have to actually put an effort into something. If you are on food stamps for the right reasons, forgive me. On the other hand, if you are on food stamps or government subsidy, you probably are not reading this book. Just for the record, this author has been on food stamps, for a length of 6 months, so don't think I don't feel your pain.

Back to the coupon warriors; is there nothing more aggravating then being behind these people at the checkout line? They delay the whole line of their fellow shoppers who are simply just trying to check-out and leave the grocery store. It is after all the middle of the week, so we all need to rush home and watch day-time TV. "The Price Is Right" and "Let's Make A Deal" is on. I must say that Drew Carey cannot hold a candle to Bob Barker. Without Monty Hall, "Let's Make A Deal" sucks, (don't ask how I know). Then to make matters worse, while we are trying to get out of the grocery store, these same people often get money back for buying groceries. The damn nerve of the coupon warrior! Why don't they just pay full price like the rest of us? I mean can you imagine, they save $200.00 and get their groceries for free? They do this in approximately two hours' time. So if grocery shopping was their career, they would be *earning* $100.00 an hour. Do you know the difference between earning $100.00 and saving $100.00? One is pre-tax, the other is after tax. I feel a financial tip coming on...

Did you know that if a 25 year old, saved $100 dollars a month for 10 years ($12,000; and could earn 8% on that money, not touch the money for an additional 30 years; there would be a total of over $175,000.00 in the account? Not to mention, if they were able to put that money in a Roth IRA, the earnings would be TAX FREE. If they put the money in a traditional IRA they would receive a tax deduction and the money would grow tax deferred. There are rules of qualification that do apply, speak with your advisor or call me. The bottom line is coupon warriors are damn cheap people who make us all late, just so they could save some money.

Of course the key word is "*saving*", as in *saving* the money you would have spent. If you spend it on something else, then you have accomplished nothing. Which means you will be associated with coupon warriors for no reason (you will ultimately lose all your friends, your dog, family members, so you might as well learn to save). Perhaps you feel as I do, "God picked my family, thank God I pick my friends." I am sure you will make new friends at the annual Coupon Cutter's Cocktail Celebration in Connecticut.

Could you imagine if you did the same thing with gas cards, reward points, and loyalty programs, as you did with coupons? You could reduce your debt, eat well, and have more family time around the kitchen table. So here is my tip. Clip coupons. Buy the things you need as opposed to want. Look for stores that take their competitor's coupons. Don't ever feel bad about saving money. The grocery chain making these offers is still making plenty of money or they would not do it. You ask how I know this to be fact. The answer is simple; they are still open for business.

Key point to remember, never use coupons for items you don't need. Let me repeat that, never use coupons for items you don't need. That would defeat the purpose. On the other hand, if the product is something you use often and has a long shelf life, then buy it.

If our great nation ever runs out of bleach or detergent, chances are we would meet as I will have the black market on those products. Just imagine, Pablo Escobar, Tony "Scarface" Montana, and David "the planner" Kossak, the kingpin of "Tide & Clorox".

So what have we learned?

1. **Coupon Warriors are human and they have feelings**
2. **Coupon Warriors are a lot smarter then we think and believe**
3. **Coupon Warriors can afford and purchase things the rest of us can't**
4. **If you can't beat them join them**
5. **The author of this cook book has lost it! ***

***Just remember who bought this cook book.**

Chapter Two
"Shop Until You Drop"

Thank the good lord we have the freedom to choose where we shop! For me, shopping at Wal-Mart is equivalent to a long treacherous death march similar to what many brave men suffered in World War Two. I don't like Wal-Mart. I despise Wal-Mart. I abhor Wal-Mart. Can you tell how I feel about Wal-Mart? Sure, they hire a lot of people, and that's great. However, it is unfortunate that many small businesses are destroyed by the arrival of this vast American employer. I just wish
The employees of Walmart did not treat you as if they were doing you a favor, (A bath or shower wouldn't hurt either)! Seriously, at the Walmart's I have been to, I would be afraid to purchase fresh fruits or vegetables for fear of contracting disease. These are my opinions, they are not facts!

A great quote which has always stuck with me has been, "Being fat, dumb and stupid is no way to go through life." This came from Dean Werner in the great movie, "*Animal House*", did I mention that I love cucumbers. I don't want you to think that I am picking on any particular income, or race of people. I respect those people who work hard, are polite, are not living on the dole, and treat their customers the same way they would want to be treated.

I mentioned income level just a second ago. The reason is my next rant is aimed at the shoppers of the grocery store called, "The Fresh Market". I call the store "The Markup Market". Sure you can eat off the floors. Yes, the employees all have skin like a *Sport's illustrated* swimsuit model. Now before you start thinking, "what location does he go to", please keep in mind I did not say they looked like swimsuit models, because if they did, I might have to reconsider my stance on this chain. I am just saying...

Seriously though, who wants to spend 5 times more for the cost of everything when you could have purchased many of the same items from a, " I have everything ever created by man store". Such as Wal-Mart. You know that would be one hell of a torture for me, save money at Walmart or go to Fresh Market. Thank god for sleeping pills and liquor.

I don't care if the Fresh Market sells prepares meals. I don't care if the meat department reminds you of where your grandfather shopped or the produce looks like it came from a corner grocer in Italy. I also don't care if the flowers, plants, candy, coffee, smells reminds you of a time long ago. The cost is ridiculous! If it's a status thing, just go ask them for a few grocery bags and keep them in your car's trunk. Then you can go shopping at another store and simply tell the other store to bag your groceries in the Fresh Markets grocery bags. When they ask, "why" tell them you are recycling your grocery bags because you care about the environment. Then when you are about to arrive home casually hit your trunk opener so your neighbors can see where you did not shop. I know what you are thinking, "PURE GENIUS".

I have discussed two completely different types of stores and experiences. The next option is a warehouse store. I know you know what I am talking about. Instead of a two for one sale, these warehouse chains have a hundred to one sale. Have you ever noticed how many fat people there are who shop there? The reason is the customer who is height challenged will buy a 64 ounce can of chili, thinking it is a single serving. I mean really, do you need to buy enough toilet paper so you don't run out before the next decade?

Most people who buy at these "membership clubs" end up throwing out much of what they buy. Unfortunately, they also throw out their fictional savings. I mean how many tomatoes can an individual eat before the tomatoes go bad. How many rib eyes will develop freezer burn, before you can finish your pack of 12? By the way, when you buy produce from one of these warehouses you better rush home. If it took you longer than an hour, the produce will probably go bad.

Before we move on, I would like to just add one last shot at these types of stores. I am going to defer to Grouch Marx when he said, "I would never join a club that would allow me to become a member." "That is all I have to say about that", Forrest Gump in the great movie Forrest Gump. Have I ever talked to you about chocolate, I love chocolate candies.

I shop at a grocery store that is part of a regional chain. The store does not sell racks of clothes, rows of tennis shoes, heavy duty tools, or patio furniture, automotive equipment, or items of a sexual nature , (with the exception of various kinds of fruits and pharmaceutical protective devices). The store chain that I am referring to, specializes in only groceries and a few necessities. In Florida, I am referring to Publix, or Winn Dixie. I would be leery of any store that was unionized, or as I like to say socialized; where an employee only has to only pee in a cup to get a pay check. There slogan is, "to hell with helping the customer, we get paid anyway!"

I love Publix. I cannot and will not cheat on "MY" Publix family by shopping anywhere else. I like my store manager and my assistant managers. I also like my cashiers, as well as baggers who range from retirees, to high school students and most importantly, "special" individuals who have to overcome more in a single day, then I will have to do in my entire life. I also like the fact that if someone is lost and looking for a particular item I can tell them where it is located. When I hear, "Thank you, do you work here?" I often reply "no, I just own this one particular Publix Market."

It is nice to be greeted by people who you are not afraid to have touched you, or who you are not afraid to shake their hands without your bottle of anti-bacteria hand sanitizer. Finally, I like it when I receive a smile from a clerk that actually has teeth, clean teeth. I find that my shopping experience can be much more pleasurable, when I am not rushed, bumped, pushed or yelled at, except by the occasional coupon Warrior.

Do you know what else I like?

I like two items for the cost of one. In other words, "buy one get one free" (BOGO). I even like "buy two get one free". I love it when I can layer the free items with my coupons; or when the coupon allows you to save a dollar on one item or two dollars on two items. Sometimes there is a competitor's store coupon to go with your manufacture's coupon as well as Publix's own in store coupons. That is equivalent to getting the items for free or there about. When that occurs, it is like I have discovered *Shangri-La*. That's me singing in the aisles!

So what have we learned?

1. You may not be saving as much as you think at your department grocery store
2. You are paying way too much at a "boutique" store
3. If you are shopping at a warehouse membership store, it is because you have not had lunch on Saturday and you know the food samples are being provided for free. Perhaps, you like large servings from a can.
4. How about shopping at a grocery store that specializes in groceries
5. Hunt for two for ones, or buy one get one frees
6. Don't forget to combine your coupons with the "two for one's"
7. You hate my sarcastic writing style*

*You still bought this cook book.

Chapter Three

"Prepare for Battle" or "Coupon Warriors Unite"

You have completed your battle plan. You have your coupons ready. You picked up a store flyer for last minute specials. You have your grocery store all picked out. Your grocery list is typed and in perfect order. You are comfortable with your choices. You have placed all your credit cards in a plastic sandwich bag, filled it with water and stuck it in the freezer. You have your debit card or this thing we at one time used to buy things with, it is called cash.

I know you want to ask about the credit cards being frozen? What are you waiting for? Okay, if you are about to make an emotional purchase (a purchase that one makes where they are happy until the return period is over, and now they have to keep the item they purchased, and every time they look at it tears come to their eyes), you are S.O.L.. The reason is your credit cards are at home and frozen so as to prevent that emotional purchase. That means that the emotional purchase has to wait until you get home and defrost your cards.

Don't even try what you are thinking of next! If you boil or nuke the sandwich bag, your cards will melt. The reason for freezing your credit cards is to make you think before you jump or purchase the un-needed item. On the other hand, in the event of an emergency—such as a car repair, an unexpected doctor or dentist visit, or even a frozen pipe explodes in your home causing it to look like Niagara Falls—you can then use your credit cards for whatever the emergency is/was.

I always shutter when I hear that a financial planner tells someone to cut up their credit cards, particularly if that person does not have 6 months of ready cash saved. Which now raises the question; does your financial advisor give you a fish, instead of teaching you how to fish? Think about that, it is very biblical.

Remember how I bragged in the foreword about feeding you and the three most important people in your life? If you do what I say, you are going to get $150.00 of groceries (minimum), for $100.00. That is almost an additional 50%.

Since we are on the subject of saving money, using Tilapia to make fish and chips with a side of hush puppies, some apple sauce on the side, a refreshing glass of iced tea and finally blueberries with Cool Whip for dessert, would cost a family of four about $16.50. Does it sounds too good to be true? Let's break it down:

The fish would cost $8.00 for four fillets. Two large Idaho potatoes would cost less than $2.50. The hush puppies are made with the left over breading or corn meal. The cost is incidental, let's say $1.50. We do need to account for the corn oil, two or three eggs to serve as the coating on the fish, prior to bread crumbs. Also, don't forget one 4 to 5 ounce container of blueberries and 4 table spoons of Cool Whip, and lastly the Ice Tea. (Bread Crumbs $0.75; three eggs $0.50; blueberries $2.50; plus $0.75 for the Cool Whip; $8.00 for the fish; $2.50 for the potatoes and $1.50 for the bread crumbs). Lunch was a large vegetable soup, a sandwich of turkey, lettuce and tomatoes, mayo on white bread with 2 ounces of chips and ice tea. The total cost to make the four lunches, less than $7.00, or $1.75 per person. Remember that the cost of the breakfast in the foreword was less than $6.00 or $1.25 per person. The total cost for the day is $20.00. I know it is $6.00 over before coupons. The coupons saved you that $6.00 dollars. Trust me!

Chapter Four

"The most important meal of the day or I love compound interest"

I have always preferred a breakfast with more substance than just a bowl of cereal. So how about breakfast with a little compound interest? Trust me, you will understand soon enough. Below are several ideas for you. There is no need to tell you how to prepare any of these meals, unless you rode the little yellow bus to school, at which point you eat for free or you work at a fast food eatery or have been elected to serve in the United States Government—particularly as a representative, senator, and of course, the big two: postal and road workers. Is there something or someone I am forgetting?

Your breakfast is up!

Breakfast Combo's (all meal plans are based on 4 people):

1. English muffin with a slice of tomato covered by a fried egg and American cheese. Place in microwave for 15 seconds if you prefer the cheese to be melted, add a sliced banana, coffee or milk. Cost: $1.75 per person
2. Peanut Butter on 2 pieces of toast. Sliced fruit, coffee, juice, or milk. Cost $1.25 per person.
3. One egg, a slice of thin ham or turkey (cooked). Toast with honey, butter, jam, sliced strawberries. Cost $1.75 per person.
4. One egg, slice of cheese, a slice of thin peppered turkey on sandwich bread two slices. Milk, juice or coffee. Cost $1.85 per person.
5. Four tablespoons of yogurt, mixed with fruit and 1 tablespoon of cereal, toast with butter and/or jam. Coffee, Milk, Juice. Cost $2.05 per person.
6. Two oatmeal cookies, four tablespoons of yogurt with fruit. Milk or coffee, and juice. Cost $1.25 per person.
7. Two scrambled eggs mixed with a one tablespoon of onions and two thin slices of smoked salmon, toast with butter. Coffee or milk or juice. Cost $2.50 per person.
8. Oatmeal with a half of cup of milk with 2 teaspoons of brown sugar. One egg with a slice of tomato. Coffee, milk or juice. Cost $1.10 per person.
9. A bowl of grits mixed with cheese, covered by two eggs, toast with butter, jam or dry. Coffee, milk and juice. Cost $1.95 per person.
10. Two egg omelet with a slice of chopped ham, tomato and onion covered by a slice of American, Swiss, or Cheddar cheese, Coffee, or milk. Cost $1.95 per person.
11. A salad with real bacon bits, crumbled hardboiled egg, shredded cheese, a tablespoon of dressing. Crackers or toast on the side. Cost $1.75 per person.
12. Cinnamon toast with butter, a side of fruit and a slice of cheese. Milk or coffee, or juice. Cost $ 1.25 per person.
13. One egg, a slice of deli sliced roast beef from package, sliced tomatoes. Coffee, Milk, or Juice, Cost $1.25 per person.

14. Buttered grits with real bacon bits, cheese and butter, sliced fruit. Milk, coffee, and juice. Cost $1.00 per person.
15. Repeat

These breakfast combos are HUGE opportunities, breakfast is the first chance to interact as a family for the day! Initially, there may be some squawking but over time it will go away. The funny thing is your friends, colleagues, and your children's friends, will be envious. Perhaps, it might even encourage them to do this with their families.

Sure it is convenient to a drive-thru and pick up one's breakfast. However, are you going to pay less than $25.00 for 4 people? The answer is "no" when you add in all the extras. The other thing that always bothers me is who touched my food while preparing it? I don't know if the cook or server just picked their nose, went to the bathroom and did not wash their hands (even though we all know about the sign or sticker that says, "ALL EMPLOYEES MUST WASH THEIR HANDS BEFORE RETURNING TO WORK").
Two problems, one, can the person who works for the fast food restaurant actually read? The second, do you really want to eat at a place that has to remind their workers to wash their hands after they wiped their tush? I am just saying, these are my opinions, not facts.

How many times have you driven away with the wrong items or something you ordered is missing? Now your day starts with frustration and anger. I understand it is more work to do it my way, but is a savings of $16.00 dollars a day worth it. You decide $16.00 a day equals $106.00 per week or $424.00 per month. If you are 40 years old, and saved that $424.00 per month in an account paying you on average of 8% per year your savings would grow to $251,463.82, at your age of 60. Did I mention the $424.00 was after tax? Even if you only do it on weekends you are still saving valuable money, you are also teaching life lessons to the children.

Most importantly, you only have your children to "rent"; God ultimately wants them to leave the nest. Why not spend a little more time together? I promise getting up 10 minutes earlier will be worth it, your children will be happier, healthier and better students. Trust me. "I have a dream"...The great MLK

Chapter Five
"Lunch the Disturbing Meal"

I have always felt that lunch was a very disturbing meal. I have been confused by lunch. It seemed odd to have a meal so close in time to breakfast, and so far in time from dinner. I also have felt after eating lunch, a good nap was in order. I always felt sorry for the person I was meeting with after lunch. My blood left my head to go to my stomach. My stomach has only come up with only one idea, and that idea had nothing to do with finances. Thank God, our office building has bathrooms. Don't you hate it when you are ready to go, and the bathroom on your floor is closed, and you have to go in the elevator or walk up or down the stairwell, just to go to a bathroom on a different floor? If you took the elevator you probably would be fine. If you took the stairs make sure the door does not lock behind you, particularly if you are on a higher floor. That could or would be trouble. I know you want to know how I know this. Let's just say I have experience.

Let go to our Lunch ideas. I left out the instructions to these meals, for the very same reason I did for the breakfast suggestions. If you are suffering from short-term memory loss, played in the NFL, and just got your concussion settlement, it was the last chapter, or the one before this one.

1. Chef Salad with a table spoon of dressing, bread or crackers, a cup of soup. Coffee, Tea, or Milk or water with a slice of lemon. Under $3.00.
2. A sandwich with any type of deli meats, lettuce, tomato, onion, a pickle, (mustard or Mayo). A few chips or a sliced tomato. Coffee, Tea, or Milk or water with a slice of Lemon. Under $2.00.
3. Tuna inside a quartered tomato, Thousand Island dressing, soup or salad, and a hard roll. Coffee, Tea, or Milk or water with a slice of Lemon. Under $ 3.00.
4. Black bean soup over rice. Texas Pete's hot sauce. Some Cuban or French bread. A cookie or two. Coffee, Tea, or Milk or water with a slice of Lemon. Under $1.50.
5. Four chicken fingers, side of ranch or hot sauce. Sliced fruit, bananas, black or blue or straw berries. Coffee, Tea, or Milk or water with a slice of Lemon. Under $2.25.
6. A piece of Mexican or American Lasagna. A side of garlic bread or corn tortillas. If Mexican Lasagna some sliced avocado. A salad for either dish. Coffee, Tea, or Milk or water with a slice of Lemon. Under a $1.00***
7. A piece of Chili Relleno Casserole. A small side salad. Coffee, Tea, or Milk or water with a slice of Lemon. Under a $1.00****
8. Tuna or Egg salad sandwiches with lettuce, tomato, a slice of cheese. A fruit salad. Coffee, Tea, or Milk or water with a slice of Lemon. Under $2.00
9. A tuna or chicken casserole. A small side salad, a hard roll, fruit salad. Coffee, Tea, or Milk or water with a slice of Lemon. Under a $1.00****

10. A Hebrew National Knockwurst, with sauerkraut or chopped onion, on bun, mustard. A citrus fruit salad. Coffee, Tea, or Milk or water with a slice of Lemon. Under $1.75.
11. Pork Chop in sauerkraut, some potato, and mustard. A brownie or cookie or pie of pie. Coffee, Tea, or Milk or water with a slice of Lemon. Under a $1.00 ****
12. A fried Tilapia sandwich, lettuce, tomato, onion. Potato chips, pickle, pie. Coffee, Tea, or Milk or water with a slice of Lemon. Under a $1.00****
13. A Blacken Chicken breast over salad, dressing, pie. Coffee, Tea, or Milk or water with a slice of Lemon. Cost $1.00*****
14. A Peanut butter and Jelly sandwich and potato chips. Coffee, Tea, or Milk or water with a slice of Lemon. Cost $1.00 (my mother's favorite)
15. Repeat

The great things about casseroles are the leftovers. The same goes for lasagna for that matter almost anything taste better the second day. The other great thing is the money we save can go to Fund College, or retirement.

I know you are waiting anxiously for the actual recipes in the "cookbook", but first another point regarding financial matters. I love going out to eat. I don't like going out to eat with colleagues particularly lunch the reason you ask; because a colleague can never become a client. If you go to a sit down restaurant, depending on where you live, you could pay as much as $50.00 just for lunch for you. I use to do it. When I think of all the money I ate, I need an Alka Seltzer. Let's say you average $20.00 plus a $5.00 tip. If you spend that amount of money four times a week that is $100.00. That equals $400.00 a month or a car payment.

On the other hand, I love taking prospects or clients to lunch. The reason is we both get out of the office and relax. The client takes their guard down and I learn a tremendous amount of information. People are very happy when they eat. I can only think of one other time people are happier, I'll leave that up to you to figure out. Sadly, as you get older that one other thing changes to, never mind. This is not an appropriate topic as I want you to be hungry not sick. It's time to prove to you, that I can cook. Let's go to dinner.

****Leftovers from a previous meal

Chapter Six

I have decided to share my 30 favorite recipes. I will be including, a picture, preparation time, actual cooking time, nutritional values, and the cost. Enjoy!

The Financial Coaches' Italian Lasagna "Bella"

Preparation: 45 minutes

Cook time: 1hour 45 minutes

Servings: 12

Cost: $2.00 per serving $24.00 for entire meal

Ingredients:

Cooking instructions:

1 lb. of lean ground beef	2 tablespoons of white sugar
½ teaspoon of fennel seeds	1 ½ teaspoons of Italian seasoning
1 lb. of sweet Italian sausage	1 tablespoon of salt
1 teaspoon of black pepper	4 tablespoons of fresh chopped Barley
½ cup minced onion	3-4 cloves of garlic, crushed
½ cup of water	2 teaspoons of basil leaves
1 can of crushed tomatoes (28 oz.)	2 cans of tomato paste (6 oz.)
2 cans of tomato sauce (6 ½ oz.)	12 Lasagna noodles (pre-cooked)
16 oz. ricotta cheese	1 egg
½ teaspoon salt	1 lb. sliced mozzarella cheese

Cook sausage and ground beef and onion in large pot over medium heat until browned. Place all tomato products and water in pot and stir. Season with Italian seasoning, basil, sugar, fennel seeds, tablespoon of salt, teaspoon of pepper and 2 tablespoons of parsley, simmer and cover for one hour and 45 minutes.

Combine ricotta cheese, egg, parsley, and ½ teaspoon of salt in a mixing bowl and mix. Preheat oven to 375 degrees F. Use a 9''x 13''baking dish. Assemble lasagna in this order; 1 ½ cups of meat sauce in bottom of baking dish, spread with ½ of the ricotta cheese mix, top with 1/3 of the mozzarella slices; place 1 ½ cups of meat sauce over mozzarella, then top with ¼ cup of parmesan cheese. Repeat process. Cover with foil, and then bake for 25 minutes. Remove foil bake for an additional 25 minutes. Let cool for 10 – 15 minutes.

Turn your thermostat up in summer, down in winter when you leave your home (10-20% savings)

The Financial Coaches' Mexican Lasagna "Bonita"

Preparation: 30 minutes

Cook time: 30 minutes

Servings: 6

Cost: $2.00 per person or $12.00 per family of four

Ingredients and measurements:

- One Pound of Lean Ground Beef or Turkey
- 12-16 corn tortillas
- a small can of Ro-tell
- ¾ cup of water
- 16 ounces of refried bean, spicy
- 1 packet of taco seasoning
- 2-4oz cans of chopped green chilies
- 2- 10 ounce cans of tortilla sauce
- 8 ounces of sour cream
- 2-8ounces of grated Mexican cheese blend

Cooking instructions:

Preheat oven to 350 degrees

Brown either beef or turkey, breaking it into crumbs

Add taco seasoning and the water, turn on low heat, let simmer for 5 minutes. Stir in green chilies and remove from heat.

Spread 2/3 cup of Enchilada sauce on bottom of 8x11, top with four corn tortillas overlap if necessary. Spread sour cream & refried beans. Then spread ½ of the turkey or ground beef, add 6 to 8 ounces of the Mexican cheese blend. Add the Rotan, for extra spice, than repeat the process. Push down on the corn tortillas. Then do the above again. Place in oven for about 30 minute. Bake uncovered, remove and serve.

An indexed mutual fund is a mirror of the index that it is tied to. In other words, an indexed mutual fund may be tied to the performance of the S & P 500, or the Russell index. Since the performance of the fund is based on the performance of the index, there is usually no investment manager thereby, reducing the loads or expenses of the fund.

The Financial Coaches' Healthy and Fast Tilapia

Preparation: 8 minutes
Cook time: 8 minutes
Servings: 4/5
Cost: $2.40 t0 $3.00 per serving, $12.00 for meal

Ingredients and measurements:

1. 4 4-5 Ounce Fillets of Tilapia
2. Salt and Pepper to your preference
3. Cajun Seasoning to your preference
4. ¾ cup of all-purpose flour
5. Spray Olive Oil
6. 2 1/4 Tablespoons of melted margarine or butter

Cooking instructions:

Rinse Tilapia fillets in cold water pat dry. Season each side of fillet with salt and pepper and Cajun spice. Place flour in a shallow tray. Dip each side of the fillet into flour. Shake off any clumps.

Spray frying pan with olive oil, heat at medium-high for 3 minutes each side or until fish flakes without effort using a fork. Brush melted margarine or butter on fillets in frying pan 1 minute prior to completion. Dinners ready, now. Team this dish with a side salad or green vegetables or both.

A typical fee for a brokerage account is 1 to 2 % per year. I have seen as high as 5 % per year from unscrupulous people. Usually, you can negotiate the fee. Never be afraid to ask.

The Financial Coaches' Mucho warm Mojo Tilapia

Preparation: 18 minutes

Cooking: 15 minutes

Servings: 4

Cost: $ 2.50 per serving

Ingredients and measurements:

- ½ cup sliced manzanilla olives
- 2 sliced red chili peppers
- 5 oz. chopped onions
- 2 packets of steamed minute rice
- 3 Tablespoons of canola oil
- 1 cup of tomato sauce
- 2 bay leaves
- ½ teaspoon of kosher salt
- ½ teaspoon pepper divided
- 4 tilapia fillets
- ½ teaspoon of adobe with pepper

Cooking instructions:

Boil rice, slice olives, cut red chili peppers into slices. Preheat saucepan on medium-high for 2-3 minutes. Add 1 tablespoon of oil, then add onions; cook until soft, 2-4 minutes. Stir in olives red chili peppers, tomato sauce, bay leaves, salt and pepper, bring to a boil. Reduce heat to medium; stir and cook 10 to 14 minutes or until vegetables are soft.

Preheat large frying pan on medium high2 to 3 minutes, season fish on both sides with adobe and pepper. Place two table spoons of oil in pan then fry fish 4 minutes each side or until fish flakes easily. Place fish on rice, add toppings. Serve.

Are you comfortable with the way your assets are invested? Are you making the decision or is your investment advisor? Your advisor should simply give you your options and his/hers unbiased opinions. Don't ever give up control. Make sure your portfolio does not keep you up at night, if it does, make appropriate changes. This is called your risk profile or tolerance level.

The Financial Coaches' Sea Food Casserole

Preparation: 5 minutes
Cook time: 45 minutes
Servings: 6
Cost: $3.00 dollars per serving; $18.00 for the recipe

Ingredients and measurements:

3 tablespoons of butter or Margarine
3 tablespoons of all-purpose flour
1 cup of whole or low fat milk
½ teaspoon of salt
1 ½ lbs. of tilapia fillets
½ lbs. of medium shrimp
½ cup of grated parmesan cheese

Cooking instructions:

Preheat oven to 325 degrees. In a small saucepan melt butter or margarine. Pour in and whisk flour and salt to make a thick paste. Gradually, wisk in milk stirring constantly.
You are done when you can coat the back of a spoon. Large casserole pan, 9 x 13, coat with cooking spray. Place fish in pan, place shrimp on top of fish. Pour in white sauce over fish and shrimp. Sprinkle grated cheese on top. Bake for 25 minutes, uncovered. Serve and enjoy.

Dollar cost averaging is a technique to put an equal amount of money into your investment on a monthly basis. To prevent the result that is often the result of a volatile swing in the stock market. It accomplishes this goal by investing a similar amount every month when the market is high or low.

The Financial Coaches' rolled "Chicken Italiano" with Pasta

Preparation: 15 to 20 minutes

Cook time: 30 minutes

Servings: 5

Cost: $2.40 per serving, $12.00 for meal

Ingredients and measurements:

5 pieces of prosciutto ham	1 to 2 oz. black or green olives	Salt and pepper
5 chicken fillets	1 tablespoon of olive oil	
1 Package of fresh basil	1 box of elbow pasta	
8 oz. whole mozzarella	3 tablespoons of grated parmesan	
3 oz. of sun dried tomatoes	¾ of teaspoon of garlic powder	

Cooking instructions:

Place strips of prosciutto ham flat, lay chicken cutlet on top of prosciutto ham, divide mozzarella into 5 slices, lay each slice flat on chicken cutlet, add fresh basil, and sun dried tomatoes, roll each one into a tight roll. Place one tablespoon of olive oil in large skillet, turn to medium high. Place each piece into skillet, and let cook until the outer part of the chicken looks done. Preheat oven to 375 degrees Then place chicken in baking tray, cook for 20 minutes or until chicken is cooked thoroughly.

Boil elbow pasta until desired softness, boil tomato sauce, add garlic powder and salt and pepper to taste, stirring frequently. Place Chicken over pasta cover with tomato sauce, add sliced black or green olives, over top. If you like you add parmesan cheese.

Exchange-traded funds*-Exchange-traded funds (ETFs) own a fixed portfolio of securities and can be bought and sold through a broker any time of the day that the stock market is open. An ETF's portfolio represents a slice of the market -- an index, a subsector of an index, or a particular industry. ETFs also come in more varieties than conventional index funds and tend to cost even less than the least costly traditional index fund. However, you have to pay a brokerage commission each time you buy or sell.*

The Financial Coaches Chili Rellenos casserole

Preparation: 15 minutes

Cook time: 45 minutes

Servings: 6

Cost: $2.00 a serving $12.00 for meal

Ingredients and measurements:

2-7 ounce cans whole green chili peppers, drained

8 ounces Longhorn or Cheddar cheese, shredded

1-5 ounce can evaporated milk

1/2 cup milk

8 ounces Monterey Jack cheese, shredded

2 eggs, beaten

2 tablespoons all-purpose flour

1 (8 ounce) can tomato sauce

Cooking instructions:

Preheat oven to 350 degrees F. Spray a 9x13-inch baking dish with cooking spray. Then lay half of the chilies evenly in bottom of baking dish, sprinkle with half of the Jack and Cheddar cheeses, and cover with remaining chilies. In a bowl, mix together the eggs, milk, and flour, and pour over the top of the chilies. Bake in the preheated oven for 25 minutes. Remove from oven, pour tomato sauce evenly over the top, and continue baking another 15 minutes. Sprinkle with remaining Jack and Cheddar cheeses, and serve.

An indexed annuity is a product created by the life insurance industry. This product allows an individual to deposit money in the accumulation value of the policy. Usually a bonus on the deposit is given. This deposit can increase the surrender charge period of the product. The return is based on the index selected. If that index drops in value, you will not lose anything, however, in return if the index increases in value, you can earn up to the companies cap. In other words, you don't get all of the winnings, because you are giving up the risk and delegating it to someone else.

The Financial Coaches' Chicken and dumplings

Preparation: 5 minutes

Cook time: 3 hour in crock pot and 15 minutes in oven.

Servings: 12

Cost: $1.75 per serving, $21.00 for meal

Ingredients and measurements:

3 large cans of Campbell's cream of chicken soup

1 large bag of Green Giant frozen mixed vegetables

5 canisters of Pillsbury instant biscuits

1 large bag of Tyson's sliced chicken breast

4 cups of water

Cooking instructions:

Place three cans of cream of chicken soup, as well as 4 cups of water. Add the vegetable and chicken breast into a crock pot. Turn on low heat for 3 hours, as long as your crock pot has an automatic warm setting, the mixture can stay in the crock pot another 3 hours.

Use a 9 x 13 baking tray; place 2 ½ of the canisters of the instant biscuits and layer the bottom of the baking tray. Add the entire mixture of soup, frozen vegetables, and chicken from the crock pot over the biscuits. Then place the remaining biscuits over the mixture of chicken, soup and vegetables. Place tray in oven at 350 degrees, until the top biscuits are brown, about 15 minutes. If you would like the biscuits on the bottom to be more firm, bake the biscuits prior to adding the mixture of soup, chicken and vegetables. Let cool for 10 minutes and serve.

It is the goal of most homeowners to pay off their mortgage as soon as possible. The reality is, your home will appreciate at the same level whether there is a mortgage on the property or not. The interest on a loan is deductible; therefore in many cases carrying a mortgage may be a good idea, particularly if you are in a high income tax bracket. NEVER BORROW OUT YOUR HOME EQUITY TO PLACE IN INVESTMENTS WHERE THERE IS RISK. You should talk to your financial advisor prior to making any decision.

The Financial coaches' chicken pot pie

Preparation: 5 minutes
Cook time: 3 hour in crock pot and 15 minutes in oven.
Servings: 12 (2 pies)
Cost: $1.75 per serving $21.00 for meal

Ingredients and measurements:

3 large cans of cream of chicken soup
1 large bag of frozen mixed vegetables
2 uncooked pie crust
1 large bag of sliced chicken breast
4 cups of water

Cooking instructions:

Place three cans of cream of chicken soup, as well as 4 cups of water. Add the vegetable and chicken breast into a crock pot. Turn on low heat for 3 hours, as long as your crock pot has an automatic warm setting, the mixture can stay in the crock pot another 3 hours.
Use a pie dish; place the bottom crust of pie in pie baking dish. Add the entire mixture of soup, frozen vegetables, and chicken from the crock pot over the pie crust. Then place the remaining pie crust over the mixture of chicken, soup and vegetables. Place Pie trays in oven at 350 degrees, until the top crust are brown, about 15 minutes. If you would like the pie crust on the bottom to be more firm, bake the bottom pie crust for 7 minutes prior to adding the mixture of soup, chicken and vegetables. Let cool for 10 minutes and serve.

Term life insurance is sold by the amount of death benefit, and the length of coverage. There is no cash value. A premium is required to keep the policy in force annually. At the end of the term period the coverage usually lapses, due to the increase of premium. Term life insurance is great for a young family with children. A term policy is much less expensive than a whole-life.

The Financial Coaches 'Clam Chowder

Preparation: 25 minutes

Cook time: 30 minutes

Servings: 6

Cost: $2.00 per serving $12.00 per meal

Ingredients and measurements:

3 (6.5 ounce) cans minced clams
1 cup minced onion
1 cup diced celery
2 cups cubed potatoes
1 cup diced carrots
3/4 cup butter
3/4 cup all-purpose flour
1 quart half-and-half cream
2 tablespoons red wine vinegar
1 1/2 teaspoons salt
ground black pepper to taste

Cooking instructions:

Drain juice from clams into a large skillet over the onions, celery, potatoes and carrots. Add water to cover, and cook over medium heat until tender.

Meanwhile, in a large, heavy saucepan, melt the butter over medium heat. Whisk in flour until smooth. Whisk in cream and stir constantly until thick and smooth. Stir in vegetables and clam juice. Heat through, but do not boil.

Stir in clams just before serving. If they cook too much they get tough. When clams are heated through, stir in vinegar, and season with salt and pepper.

When grocery shopping, only buy what you need. Bring a list. Do not impulse buy, even if something looks like a good price or sale. You will save a tremendous amount of money. Think family vacation!

The Financial Coaches Blackened Chicken

Preparation: 10 minutes

Cook Time: 10 minutes

Servings: 4

Cost: $1.25 per serving $5.00 per meal

Ingredients and measurements

1 teaspoon paprika

¼ teaspoon salt

½ cayenne peppers

½ teaspoon ground cumin

½ teaspoon dried thyme

¼ teaspoon ground white pepper

¼ teaspoon onion powder

4 chicken breast

Cooking Instructions:

Preheat oven to 350 degrees. Lightly grease a baking sheet. Heat a cast iron skillet over high heat for 5 minutes until it is smoking hot.

Mix together the paprika, salt, cayenne, cumin, thyme, white pepper, and onion powder. Oil the chicken breasts with cooking spray on both sides, and then coat the chicken breasts evenly with the spice mixture.

Place the chicken in the hot pan, and cook for 1 minute. Turn, and cook 1 minute on other side. Place the breasts on the prepared baking sheet.

Bake in the preheated oven until no longer pink in the center and the juices run clear, about 5 minutes.

Whole life insurance is a very expensive way to purchase life insurance. The life insurance company inflates the premium. They then issue dividends, which the IRS defines as an overcharge of premiums. These dividends grow tax free. However, any interest earned on the dividend is taxable. The cash value grows over the insured's lifetime. This cash value can be used for anything. The cash value has to be taken out in the form of a loan. The dividends can be withdrawn by simply surrendering them. Whole life is a good product for anyone who does not need a lot of life insurance and is looking for a means to put money away. The other individual whom this product would be great for is someone who can afford to save a lot of money and is conservative.

The Financial Coaches Blackened Tilapia

Preparation: 10 minutes

Cook Time: 6 minutes

Servings: 4

Cost: $1.25 per serving $5.00 per meal

Ingredients and measurements

1 teaspoon paprika

¼ teaspoon salt

½ cayenne peppers

½ teaspoon ground cumin

½ teaspoon dried thyme

¼ teaspoon ground white pepper

¼ teaspoon onion powder

4 Tilapia Fillets

Cooking Instructions:

Heat a cast iron skillet over high heat for 5 minutes until it is smoking hot.

Mix together the paprika, salt, cayenne, cumin, thyme, white pepper, and onion powder. Oil the chicken breasts with cooking spray on both sides, and then coat the chicken breasts evenly with the spice mixture.

Place the Tilapia in the hot pan, and cook for 2-3 minute. Turn, and cook 2-3 minute on other side. Add a side salad or green vegetables.

Serve.

One of the biggest mistakes that anyone can make is overlapping the investments in their 401-k. Overlapping means choosing mutual funds within the 401-k that have the same or similar holdings. Thereby negatively affecting the diversification of the portfolio.

The Financial Coaches' Blackened Steak

Preparation: 10 minutes
Cook Time: 20 minutes
Servings: 4
Cost: $6.00 per serving $24.00 per meal

Ingredients and measurements

1 teaspoon paprika
¼ teaspoon salt
½ cayenne peppers
½ teaspoon ground cumin
½ teaspoon dried thyme
¼ teaspoon ground white pepper
¼ teaspoon onion powder
4 ½ to ¾ pound steaks

Cooking Instructions:

Preheat oven to 350 degrees. Lightly grease a baking sheet. Heat a cast iron skillet over high heat for 5 minutes until it is smoking hot.

Mix together the paprika, salt, cayenne, cumin, thyme, white pepper, and onion powder. Oil the chicken breasts with cooking spray on both sides, and then coat the Steaks evenly with the spice mixture.

Place the steak in the hot pan, and cook for 1 1/2 minutes. Turn, and cook 1 1/2 minute on other side. Place the steaks on the prepared baking sheet.

Bake in the preheated oven for about 5 minutes.

Do you think income taxes will be at higher rate at your retirement or lower? If you think they will be higher than a good idea is to only contribute to your 401-k plan up to the match by your company. Take the after tax amount that you would have put into the 401-k and place that in a Roth IRA or a life insurance product. With either one there are ways to withdraw the money and growth tax free.

The Financial Coaches' Breaded Pork Chop W/ Brown Gravy

Preparation: 15 minutes
Cook time: 1 hour 15 minutes
Servings: 6
Cost: $2.75 per serving $16.50

Ingredients and measurements:

1 tablespoon butter
1 clove garlic, pressed
6 pork chops
salt and pepper to taste
1 (8 ounce) can mushrooms, drained
1 cup dry sherry
1 (10.5 ounce) can beef broth
2 tablespoons cornstarch
2 tablespoons water

Cooking instructions:

Preheat the oven to 350 degrees
Melt the butter in a large skillet over medium heat. Add garlic, and sauté until fragrant. Season pork chops with salt and pepper, then fry them in the skillet just until browned on both sides, about 3 minutes per side. Remove the pork chops to a baking pan or Dutch oven. Pour the mushrooms into the skillet with the pork drippings and garlic, and stir in the sherry and beef broth, scraping any bits of pork that are stuck to the pan. Bring to a boil, and then pour over the pork chops in the baking pan. Cover with a lid, or aluminum foil. Bake for 45 minutes in the preheated oven, then remove the lid or foil, and continue to bake for another 15 minutes. Remove the chops from the pan to a serving platter, and place the dish on the stove over medium heat. Stir together the cornstarch and water. When the juices in the pan come to a boil, slowly stir in the cornstarch mixture and cook until thickened, about 2 minutes. Spoon sauce over the chops, and serve.

Many new retires want to take a large sum out of their retirement assets, to purchase something frivolous. It's called "YOLO money"—you only live once." I'm the first guy to say go out and enjoy yourself early on—you aren't going to get any healthier." However, do not be tempted to purchase an item that will throw your entire retirement strategy in chaos. I have seen this done. A moment of instant gratification effects your entire retirement negatively. THINK!

The Financial Coaches' Tuna "Sorry Charlie" Patties

Preparation: 15 minutes
Cook time: 10 minutes
Servings: 4
Cost: $1.50 per serving $6.00 per meal

Ingredients and measurements:

2 eggs
1/4 cup grated Parmesan cheese
3/4 cup seasoned bread crumbs
1 to 3 teaspoons of lemon juice
3 (6 ounce) cans tuna, drained
1/4 cup diced onion
1 pinch ground black pepper
3 tablespoons olive oil

Cooking instructions:

Beat eggs and lemon juice in a bowl; stir in Parmesan cheese and bread crumbs to make a paste. Fold in tuna and onions until well-mixed. Season with black pepper. Shape tuna mixture into eight 1-inch-thick patties.

Heat olive oil in a skillet over medium heat; fry patties until golden brown, 4 minutes each side.

Create a second e-mail address for only coupons, loyalty clubs, reward clubs, etc. That way you won't have confusion when you focus on saving offers. Do not have that e-mail address on your smart phone. You will be inundated all day .This technique will save you time and money and reduce stress.

Financial Coaches Beef Stew

Preparation: Few minutes

Cook time: 12 hours

Servings: 6

Cost: $1.15 $6.90 for meal

Ingredients and measurements:

4 carrots, chopped
3 potatoes, peeled and cubed
2 onion, chopped
3 stalks celery, chopped
1 cup sliced fresh mushrooms
3 pounds cubed stew meat
1 packet dry onion soup mix
2 cups water
1 (10.75 ounce) can condensed golden mushroom soup

Cooking instructions:

Place the carrots, potatoes, mushrooms, onion and celery in the slow cooker. Place the stew meat over the vegetables. In a medium bowl, combine the soup mix with the can of soup. Add the water and mix together well. Pour this in the slow cooker over the meat and vegetables. Add water as needed so that the liquid comes just to the bottom of the meat. Cook on low for 12 hours. Add water if necessary.

In retirement, a major, unexpected expense can quickly send a financial plan off the rails. But that doesn't have to happen. I see a lot of people cutting it really close and living paycheck to paycheck, even though they are really paying themselves" out of their savings. The problem comes when an emergency crops up that requires laying out extra cash on short notice. If that outlay requires selling investments in the middle of a market downturn, the retiree could be locking in losses that can't be recovered. It takes planning ahead. I advise my clients to keep six months to one year's worth of cash on hand for replenishing that stockpile.

The Financial Coaches Lox and Eggs and Onions (Breakfast for dinner)

Preparation: 5 minutes

Cook: 5 minutes

Servings: 4

Cost: $1.50 serving 6 meal

Ingredients & measurements

6 teaspoons flavorless vegetable oil

1 1/2 cup thinly sliced yellow onion

Kosher or sea salt and black pepper

6 extra-large eggs, lightly beaten

Water Bagel with cream cheese

6 ounces smoked salmon

6 teaspoons unsalted butter

3 generous tablespoon thinly sliced, fresh chives

Cooking Instructions:

Heat an 8-inch nonstick skillet over medium-high heat, add the vegetable oil. When the oil is hot, add the onion and cook, stirring frequently, until softened, Sprinkle the onion with a little salt and black pepper and scrape into a small bowl. Sauté the salmon over medium-high heat, stirring frequently, just until it loses its translucency, about 30 seconds. Add the salmon to the bowl of hot onion. When hot add the beaten eggs and turn the heat to medium. Let the eggs cook,

Other stock-fund categories are sector funds, which invest in a single industry or economic sector; balanced funds, whose assets include large percentages of both stocks and bonds; and utility funds, which invest in income-heavy utility stocks.

The Financial Coaches' Chopped Salad

Preparation Time: 25 minutes

Servings: 4

Cost: $5.00 per serving $20.00 per meal

Ingredients and measurements:

Blend 1/3 cup **feta**
2 tablespoons **olive oil**,
1 small grated **garlic clove**
1 chopped **romaine heart**
1 small chopped **cucumber**,
1 tablespoon water
5 chopped **radishes**
1 tablespoon **lemon juice**
1 tablespoon of dill
1 Chopped Green, Red, and Yellow Pepper

Toss Season with salt and pepper.

"There's no such thing as a free lunch." That's especially the case with investments promising big payoffs with low risk. People "have a unique ability to suspend common sense, believing that strangers want to let us in on deals that are too good to be true, which of course, are," There are often telltale signs it's time to hang up the phone on a sales pitch. They include: a sense of urgency ("The deal is only good today!"), using a church or fraternal organization to vouch for its credibility or a play on emotions.

The Financial Coaches' Sesame Flank Steak

Preparation: 10 minutes;
Cook time: 12 minutes
Servings: 4
Cost: $ 3.00 a serving $12.00 for meal

Ingredients and measurements:

1/3 cup of sesame seed oil
¼ cup of sugar
2 cloves of garlic or 1 teaspoon
2-inch piece of fresh ginger root or teaspoon
1 large cucumber
1 cup of matchstick carrots
2lb. beef flank steak
3 tablespoons of sesame seeds
½ cup of soy sauce
½ teaspoon crushed red peppers
large zip-top bag
½ cup pre-sliced green onion

Cooking instructions:

Place all ingredients in zip-top bag, seal bag and squeeze or turn upside down to right side up to blend mixture add steak to bag. The longer you can marinate the better. The minimum is 30 minutes.
Preheat large skillet to medium high 3 minutes. Place steak on grill turning every 30 seconds, repeat for 12 minutes. Place remaining contents of zip-top bag in a small sauce pan and bring to a boil. Remove steak let stand for 5 minutes. Slice diagonally against the grain of the steak, Sprinkle remaining sauce on steak and serve.
White rice go's great with this recipe, as does a salad with ginger dressing.

The "no free lunch" risk to a nest egg also applies to investors who have cut back on holdings of relatively safe but low-yielding government bonds and bulked up on riskier investments that offer meatier yields—like high-yielding junk bonds, bank-loan funds or dividend-paying stocks. When you substitute a fixed-income, low-volatility investment for a higher-volatility investment, the risk of a loss of principal in a down market is much higher.

The Financial Coaches' Red Curry Flank Steak

Preparation: 5 minutes

Cook time: 1 hour 10 minutes

Servings: 4

Cost: $2.00 per serving 8 per meal

Ingredients and measurements:

1/4 cup seasoned rice vinegar
3 tablespoons fish sauce
2" piece freshly grated ginger, tablespoon
4 cloves garlic, crushed
2 teaspoon hot sauce
1 teaspoon red curry powder
1 teaspoon red curry paste
1-2 lb. flank steak
1 bunch fresh basil

Cooking instructions:

Whisk rice vinegar, fish sauce, grated ginger, garlic, hot sauce, red curry powder, and red curry paste in a shallow dish. Set aside. Puncture flank steak several times with a fork and place in the vinegar mixture. Cover and marinate at room temperature for 1 hour. Preheat an outdoor grill for high heat, and lightly oil the grate. Place steak on the grill and basil on top of steak. Grill steak for 6 minutes. Remove basil, turn meat over, and place basil back on top of steak. Cook the steak until it begins to firm and is hot and slightly pink in the center

"Acting emotionally in a down market could be mistake No. 1" when it comes to wrecking a nest egg, Retirees who need their savings to help pay the bills will feel the pull of reacting to short-term losses. "During retirement, its behavioral economics on steroids," Retirees should build a portfolio that meets their long-term goals and one where they can withstand watching the inevitable downs in the markets that come with the ups. To put it another way, the FC says: "It's dumb to buy high and sell low."

The Financial Coaches' Salmon Especial

Preparation: 10 Minutes
Cook Time: 30 minutes
Servings: 4
Cost: $3.00 serving $12.00 meal

Ingredients and measurements

2 salmon steaks
salt and pepper to taste
6 tablespoons cooking oil, divided
2 onion, chopped
4 cloves garlic, crushed
4 tomatoes, diced
2 egg, beaten

Cooking

Season both sides of the salmon steaks with salt and pepper. Heat 5 tablespoons cooking
Oil in a skillet over medium heat. Briefly fry the salmon in hot oil until lightly cooked, about 3 minutes per side. Remove from skillet and set aside. Add 1 tablespoon cooking oil to the skillet and allow getting hot before adding the onion and garlic; cooking and stirring the onion and garlic in the hot oil until onion is clear, about 5 minutes. Stir the diced tomatoes into the mixture and season with salt and pepper. Continue cooking until the moisture from the tomatoes makes a sauce, about 5 minutes more. Return the salmon to the skillet and allow simmering in the sauce until the fish flakes easily with a fork, about 10 minutes. Stir the beaten egg into the sauce and stir until well integrated; serve hot.

A tax Free Retirement plan funded with Life Insurance is a very good way to protect assets from creditors in most states. This retirement plans guarantees your family what is supposed to be in the retirement plan will be there, in the event of disability or death. The money can be accessed from the policy by loans, which allows the recipient to receive withdrawal tax free.

The Financial Coaches Extraordinary Lamb

Preparation: 25-35 minutes

Cook: 2hours 15 Minutes

Servings: 6 (2 will be used for lunch or another meal)

Cost: $4.50 serving $27.00

Ingredients and measurements

6 lamb shanks
salt and pepper to taste
2 tablespoons olive oil
2 onions, chopped
3 large carrots, cut into 1/4 inch rounds
10 cloves garlic, minced
1 (750 milliliter) bottle red Wine
1 (28 ounce) can whole peeled tomatoes with juice
1 (10.5 ounce) can condensed chicken broth
1 (10.5 ounce) can beef broth
5 teaspoons chopped fresh rosemary
2 teaspoons chopped fresh thyme

Cooking:

Sprinkle shanks with salt and pepper. Heat oil in heavy large pot over medium-high heat. Working in batches, cook shanks until brown on all sides, about 8 minutes. Transfer shanks to plate. Add onions, carrots and garlic to pot and sauté until golden brown, about 10 minutes. Stir in wine, tomatoes, chicken broth and beef broth. Season with rosemary and thyme. Return shanks to pot, pressing down to submerge. Bring to a boil, and then reduce heat to medium-low. Cover, and simmer until meat is tender, about 2 hours. Remove cover from pot. Simmer about 20 minutes longer. Transfer shanks to platter, place in a warm oven. Boil juices in pot until thickened, about 15 minutes. Spoon over shanks.

In simplest terms, mutual funds fall into two broad groupings: stock funds and bond funds in general, stock funds deliver greater returns over the long term than bond funds. But stock funds are less predictable and more likely to deliver sharp losses as well as gains over relatively short spans of time, leaving short-term investors unsure of how much they'll have when they need their money.

The Financial Coaches Lamb Chops

Preparation: 10 Minutes
Cook: 2hours 6 Minutes
Servings: 6 (2 will be used for lunch or another meal)
Cost: $4.50 serving $27.00

Ingredients and measurements

1/4 cup distilled white vinegar
2 teaspoons salt
1/2 teaspoon black pepper
1 tablespoon minced garlic
1 onion, thinly sliced
2 tablespoons olive oil
2 pounds lamb chops

Cooking:

Mix together the vinegar, salt, pepper, garlic, onion, and olive oil in a large reseal-able bag until the salt has dissolved. Add lamb, toss until coated, and marinate in refrigerator for 2 hours.
Preheat Broiler Remove lamb from the marinade and leave any onions on that stick to the meat. Discard any remaining marinade. Wrap the exposed ends of the bones with aluminum foil to keep them from burning. Grill to desired doneness, about 3 minutes per side for medium. The chops may also be broiled in the oven about 5 minutes per side for medium.

Stock funds rely on their holdings to rise in value in order to deliver good returns. Bond funds achieve much of their return by collecting interest on the securities they own. Stock funds are divided this way:
Aggressive growth-These strive for big profits, generally by investing in small companies and developing industries or by concentrating on volatile issues. The greater the drive for high profits, the greater the risk
Growth and income-These funds have much the same objective as growth funds, but they put greater emphasis on capital preservation and try to produce more current dividend income for shareholders. These funds invest in bonds, preferred stocks, and high-yielding common stocks.
Index funds-These assemble portfolios designed to track as precisely as possible one or more broad stock or bond index. Funds that track the Standard & Poor's 500 are perhaps the best known, but there are many others.
International funds-International funds are U.S.-based but invest in securities of companies traded on foreign exchanges. They are good places to be when the value of the dollar is falling.

The Financial Coaches' Pork Roast

Preparation: 25 minutes

Cook: 2hours

Servings: 6 (2 will be used for lunch or another meal)

Cost: $2.50 serving $15.00

Ingredients and measurements

3 pounds pork tenderloin

1 tablespoon olive oil

2 cloves garlic, minced

3 tablespoons dried rosemary

Cooking:

Preheat oven to 375 degrees Rub the roast OR tenderloin liberally with olive oil, then spread the garlic over it. Place it in a 10x15 inch roasting pan and sprinkle with the rosemary. Bake at 375 degrees F for 2 hours, or until the internal temperature of the pork reaches 145 degrees F

This tip is very appropriate for the food choice, "pork". Throughout my career, (34 years). I have heard most everything that one could hear in regards to financial planning. From floating Dairy Farms to exotic off shore ventures." Baskin Robbins may have 31 flavors of ice cream, but vanilla has been around a long time. It has survived the likes of "bear and otter claws ice cream. There is a reason why, and Baskin Robbins knows that reason. History, tradition, nothing fancy, just plain vanilla. I look at planning the same way. Get it.

The Financial Coach's Spicy Sweet Asian Salmon

Preparation: 10 minutes

Cook: 27 minutes

Serves: 4

Cost: $3.00 serving $12.00 meal

Ingredients and Measurements:

1.75 lb. of fresh Salmon (four fillets)

Soy Sauce (low sodium)

Teriyaki Sauce

Sweet Chili Sauce

Texas Pete's Hot Sauce

Directions:

Combine 1 tablespoon of soy sauce with 1.5 Tablespoons of sweet chili Sauce and 1 tablespoon of Teriyaki sauce and 1 teaspoon of Texas Pete's, stir together in a small bowl. Use a 9"x 13" baking pan. Spray with olive oil. Place the four fillets in pan. Place the skin side down. Brush sauce on salmon. Preheat oven to 375 degrees. Place salmon in over, bake for 15 minutes and reapply additional sauce, and bake for an additional 10 minutes. Apply remaining sauce and bake for 2 minutes. The Salmon should be a light orange in middle of fillet.

Add rice and salad.

This cookbook has a tremendous diversification of recipes. There are many different combinations. Not any one recipe is the same as another, in other words there is no overlapping of foods. Isn't it interesting to note, that the most successful investor, is one who has tremendous diversification, his portfolio does not have any two investment that are alike, and there is no overlapping of investments within the portfolio. Financial planning is not rocket science; it is common sense.

The Financial Coach's Osso Buco

Preparation: 20 minutes

Cook: 2 hour 27 minutes

Serves: 8

Cost: $7.00 serving $56.00 meal (every once in a while you have to splurge, 4 extra)

Ingredients and Measurements:

1/4 cup all-purpose flour

2 cloves garlic, crushed

1 (8 ounce) can tomato sauce

8 pounds veal shank

1 cup water

1 teaspoon dried thyme

1 bay leaf

1 cup chopped onion

1/2 cup chopped celery

2 teaspoons salt

1/4 teaspoon ground black pepper

3 tablespoons butter

1 teaspoon dried basil

3 sprigs fresh parsley

3 tablespoons olive oil

1 cup thinly sliced carrots

Directions:

In a shallow dish, stir together flour, salt, and black pepper. Dredge meat in seasoned flour. In a large skillet, melt butter with oil over medium heat. Brown meat. Remove meat from pan, and set aside. Add onion, carrots, celery, and garlic to drippings in pan. Cook and stir for about 5 minutes. Stir in tomato sauce, water, basil, thyme, parsley, and bay leaf. Return meat to pan. Bring to a boil, and reduce heat to simmer. Cover, and cook for 2 1/2 hours.

Due the cost and the time constraint I make this recipe only once or twice a year. Nonetheless, sometimes you just have to enjoy your life. If everything goes towards savings, then you are going to wake up one day old poor. There is nothing wrong with using this, my favorite as a goal to accomplish your objectives. If I save 20% this month, I am going to reward myself with this wonderful dish. There is nothing wrong with goal setting. So, rather than abstract goals, determine what habits you'll need to adopt in order to gradually improve your financial situation. Osso Buco is an incentive that will prevent you from abandoning your quest prior to fulfillment.

The Financial Coach's Chicago Doggie

Preparation: 10 minutes

Cook: 27 minutes

Serves: 4

Cost: $1.75 serving $7.00 meal

Ingredients and Measurements:

4 Seeded & Roasted Onion Bun
2 oz. Yellow mustard
4 oz. sweet pickle relish
8 tomatoes slices
Dash celery salt
4 Hebrew National Knockwurst
2 oz. white onion, chopped
4 dill pickle spear
8 pickled sport peppers

Directions:

Boil Hebrew National Knockwurst in a can of beer. When done, remove knockwurst place Seeded & Roasted Onion Bun, then place remaining ingredients on knockwurst. Enjoy. Add potato chips

WHAT IS BETTER THEN SIMPLE AND EASY TO UNDERSTAND AND ENJOY! "Only two in five adults maintain a budget and keep close track of their spending, according to the National Foundation for Credit Counseling, and that ratio has remained the same since 2007. It's therefore no surprise that U.S. consumers have racked up tens of billions of dollars in credit card debt since then. Fortunately, the rise in online money management tools makes expense and payment tracking easier than ever. Supplemental strategies, like the Island Approach or asking your credit card issuer to lower your spending limit to match your budget, are conducive to the adoption of sustainable spending and payment habits as well. Ultimately, your budget should reflect your annual financial goals and effectively serve as a roadmap for achieving them."

The Financial Coaches Chili Pork

Preparation: 10 minutes

Cook: 2hours 15 Minutes

Servings: 12

Cost: $3.50 serving $26.00 (8 will be used for lunch or another meal)

Ingredients & Measurements

2 tablespoons chili powder
1 teaspoon salt
2 1/2 teaspoons ground cumin
2 teaspoons minced garlic
1 tablespoon fresh cilantro
2 pounds pork tenderloin, cubed
1 dash ground black Pepper

Cooking

Mix together: chili powder, salt, cumin, garlic Cilantro and pepper. Coat pork cubes with mixture and let sit for 45 minutes in refrigerator
Preheat oven to 225 degrees. Bake 2 hours, or until crispy.

Whatever happened to the word "good"? Did it get lost in the world Of "great"? The truth is, you can be good a lot longer than you can Be great. We have moments of greatness, but there is something To a lifetime of good. Investments are that way too, you have the craze of a new fad, like a dot com; or you can have the stability of a Proven long standing company that has been "good". So be good Feel good, Be good and Do well!

The Financial Coach's Holy Romano Chicken

Preparation: 15 minutes
Cook: 4 minutes
Serves: 4
Cost: $3.00 serving $12.00 meal

Ingredients and Measurements:

1/4 pound Swiss cheese, sliced
1 Tablespoons grated Parmesan cheese
1/2 teaspoon garlic salt
1/2 teaspoon dried basil leaves
1/3 cup dry bread crumbs
1/4 pound ham, sliced thin
2 teaspoons paprika
1/2 teaspoon dried tarragon
1 tablespoon butter, melted
6 Chicken Fillets

Directions:

Place chicken breasts on a pan. Place Swiss cheese and ham slices on top and roll up, securing with toothpicks if necessary. In a small bowl combine the Parmesan cheese, paprika, garlic salt, tarragon, basil and bread crumbs. Mix together and dip rollups in mixture to coat. Drizzle with melted butter and cook on High in microwave for 4 minutes, or until chicken is cooked through and juices run clear.

"Show me a person who has no room to save on their monthly bills and I'll show you a fool. From cell phone contracts and premium cable packages to groceries and utility payments, we all have some budget fat than could stand to be cut. So, put all of your accounts and habits on the table in the New Year, determine whether or not you are getting the best possible deals, and adjust accordingly

The Financial Coach's Sesame Seed Chicken

Preparation: 15 minutes

Cook: 15 minutes

Serves: 6

Cost: $3.00 serving $18.00 meal (2 extra meals)

Ingredients and Measurements:

1/2 cup toasted sesame seeds, divided
1 teaspoon sweet pepper sauce
5 skinless, chicken breast cut into chunks
1/2 yellow onion, cut into wedges
1 cup all-purpose flour
2 tablespoons honey
1 teaspoon black pepper
1 teaspoon crushed red pepper flake
5 tablespoons vegetable oil
1/2 cup green bell pepper
2 tablespoons teriyaki sauce

Directions:

Get a large resalable plastic bag, combine flour, 1/4 cup sesame seeds, black pepper, five-spice powder, and red pepper flakes. Place a few pieces of chicken at a time into the bag, and shake to coat. Remove to a platter; heat oil in a large skillet or wok over medium-high heat. Place chicken into skillet, and brown on both sides, about 5 minutes. Remove chicken, and set aside. Stir onion wedges and bell pepper slices into skillet; cook until slightly browned, about 2 minutes. Remove, and set aside. Return chicken to skillet, and reduce heat to low. Mix in teriyaki marinade, 1/4 cup sesame seeds, and honey; stir until sauce thickens. Return onion and bell pepper to the skillet. Warm through, and serve.

"The Great Recession taught us a number of important lessons about strategic financial planning as well as the value of cash reserves. Now is the time to apply what we've learned. So, if you don't have an emergency fund, a retirement fund AND a college fund for your kids, open them up and get to saving. Your goal should be to end the year with 10 percent more money in each of these accounts, so make sure to factor that into your budget. And while it may surprise many people, establishing an emergency fund is actually a higher priority than paying off debt because without cash reserves, you'll only be an unexpected expense or income disruption away from ending up right back where you started, even if you manage to get out of debt in the short term

The Financial Coach's Chicken Curry

Preparation: 15 minutes
Cook: 20 minutes
Serves: 8
Cost: $3.00 serving $24.00 meal (4 servings left over)

Ingredients and Measurements:

1/2 cup and 2 table spoons of Panang curry paste
12 kaffir lime leaves, torn
1/2 cup fresh Thai basil leaves
8 cups coconut milk
1/4 cup palm sugar
1/4 cup fish sauce, or to taste
4 fresh red chili peppers, sliced
cooking oil
1-1/4 pounds skinless, chicken breast, cubed

Directions:

Fry the curry paste in the oil in a large skillet or wok over medium heat until fragrant. Stir the coconut milk into the curry paste and bring to a boil. Add the chicken; cook and stir until the chicken is nearly cooked through, 10 to 15 minutes. Stir the palm sugar, fish sauce, and lime leaves into the mixture; simmer together for 5 minutes. Taste and adjust the saltiness by adding more fish sauce if necessary. Garnish with sliced red chili peppers and Thai basil leaves to serve.
Add rice

"Investment management is a full-time job, and even the pros regularly make mistakes. It's therefore important to ask yourself if you have the time, inclination, and knowledge base to actively manage your own investment portfolio. For the average person, the answer to those questions is likely to be no, which means a portfolio comprised of well-diversified ETFs and mutual funds is the way to go. After all, only 24 percent of professional investors beat the market in the last decade.

The Financial Coach's Chicken Alfredo & Broccoli

Preparation: 10 minutes

Cook: 12 minutes

Serves: 4

Cost: $3.00 serving $12.00 meal

Ingredients and Measurements:

8 ounces fettuccine or spaghetti, uncooked

1/4 cup Zesty Italian Dressing

1 2/3 cups milk

1/4 cup Grated Parmesan Cheese

2 cups fresh broccoli florets

1 pound boneless skinless chicken breasts cut, bite-sized

4 ounces PHILADELPHIA Cream Cheese, cubed

1/2 teaspoon dried basil leaves

Directions:

Cook pasta as directed on package, adding broccoli to the boiling water for the last 2 min. of the pasta cooking time. Drain pasta mixture. Heat dressing in large nonstick skillet on medium-high heat. Add chicken; cook 5 min. or until chicken is cooked through, stirring occasionally. Stir in milk, cream cheese, Parmesan cheese and basil. Bring to boil, stirring constantly. Cook 1 to 2 min. or until sauce is well blended and heated through; add chicken mixture to pasta mixture;

Financial awareness is much more than investing. It's the key to responsible money management. Don't let history repeat itself; we have been through the Great Recession. We have a responsibility to instill in our children the value of a dollar; as well as the importance of saving. We must also practice what we preach. It is up to you to gain financial knowledge, and apply what you have learned to your money management strategies.

I know you did not believe me, when I said I could cook, but I have to ask, "What do you think of me NOW!" The truth is I'll put my recipes up against anyone, anytime, and any place. I can assure all of you," that you can do it" The Water boy" with the great Adam Sandler".

Cooking is not rocket science, neither is Financial Planning.

Chapter 7
"Getting you Just Deserts"

My father would not leave the table until my mother served him the dessert. Unfortunately, for all of us, we never had a homemade desert. My mother would serve us Sara Lee right out of the aluminum tray. No ambience, nothing fancy, just frozen desserts! Ooh it made me wonder... Ooh it really made me wonder, a new day will dawn for those who will stay long. There is a place where you can stuff your face and the only way to get there is The Stairway to Heaven." Led Zeppelin" please forgive me!
Love desserts. I never knew how much fun it was to bake, and experiment; Trying to make a very caloric deserts low cal. I learned that Splenda bakes similar to sugar. I do add a little cinnamon, as the Splenda is slightly sweeter than sugar. You have your choice, try both ways to bake and determine for yourself. Don't forget many of the deserts use fresh fruit, thus giving a more natural sweet taste. I am not including any cost, as you will see by reading the ingredients you will be well within your budget.
I cannot think of anything more American then Apple Pie, that is where I want to begin. Enjoy The Financial Coaches top ten desserts, (where is David Letterman when you need him).

The Financial Coaches' "Ode to our Grandmothers" Apple Pie
Ingredients and Measurements:

Pre-made un-cocked pie crust 1/2 cup white sugar or Splenda
1/2 cup packed brown sugar or ½ of Tablespoon of cinnamon
Granny Smith apples peeled/ sliced 1/2 cup unsalted butter
3 tablespoons all-purpose flour 1/4 cup water

Directions:

Preheat oven to 425 degrees. Melt the butter in a saucepan. Stir in flour to form a paste. Add water, white sugar and brown sugar, and bring to a boil. Reduce temperature and let simmer. Place the bottom crust in your pan. Fill with apples, mounded slightly. Cover with a lattice work crust. Gently pour the sugar and butter liquid over the crust. Pour slowly so that it does not run off. Bake 15 minutes in the preheated oven. Reduce the temperature to 350 degrees F. Continue baking for 35 to 45 minutes, until apples are soft. Don't forget the alamode.

When was the last time you reviewed your budget? How well have you been sticking to it? Simplify your budget. Don't let it become an obsession. You will then be more likely to follow it.

The Financial Coaches amazing Blueberry Pie

Ingredients and Measurements:

4 cups fresh blueberries 1 recipe pastry for a 9 inch double crust pie
1 tablespoon butter 3/4 cup white sugar
3 tablespoons cornstarch 1/4 teaspoon salt
1/2 teaspoon ground cinnamon

Cooking Directions:

Preheat oven to 425 degrees F.
Mix sugar, cornstarch, salt, and cinnamon, place in a plastic bag, then place blueberries in plastic bag. Shake bag gently until blueberries are covered with mix; line pie dish with one pie crust. Pour berry mixture into the crust, and dot with butter. Cut remaining pastry into 1/2 - 3/4 inch wide strips, and make lattice top; next, Crimp and flute edges with a fork. Bake pie on lower shelf of oven for about 50 minutes, or until crust is golden brown.

Get rid of accounts that you are not usings. ***If you have multiple bank accounts, consider closing some, particularly if you hardly ever use them.***
What about retirement accounts from a former employer or more than one IRA account, consider combining them. Unless you enjoy paying twice as much in fees.

The Financial Coaches' "World Famous" Strawberry Pie

Ingredients and Measurements:

1 recipe pastry for a 9 inch single crust pie
3/4 cup white sugar
3/4 cup all-purpose flour
6 tablespoons butter
1 pinch ground nutmeg
4 cups fresh strawberries, hulled
1 tablespoon cornstarch
1/2 cup all-purpose flour
1/2 cup white sugar

Cooking Directions:

Preheat oven to 425 degrees F.
Mix sugar, cornstarch, salt, and cinnamon, place in a plastic bag, then place blueberries in plastic bag. Shake bag gently until blueberries are covered with mix; line pie dish with one pie crust. Pour berry mixture into the crust, and dot with butter. Cut remaining pastry into 1/2 - 3/4 inch wide strips, and make lattice top; next, Crimp and flute edges with a fork. Bake pie on lower shelf of oven for about 50 minutes, or until crust is golden brown.

I usually hear a few times a week, "I am going to get a large tax refund". What that means to me is you lent the government money tax free. I don't think the IRS allows you to pay them over time without interest and in some cases penalties.
Adjust your withholdings appropriately.

The Financial Coaches' "Georgia" Peach Pie

Ingredients and Measurements:

1 (9 inch) pie shell, baked
1 cup white sugar
1/2 cup water
3 tablespoons cornstarch
1 tablespoon butter
2 cups fresh peaches, pitted and mashed
1/4 teaspoon ground nutmeg
1 teaspoon vanilla extract
4 cups fresh peaches - pitted, skinned, and sliced

Cooking Directions:

Combine sugar, water, cornstarch, butter or margarine, mashed peaches, and nutmeg in a saucepan. Cook over medium heat until clear and thick. Stir in vanilla. Fill pie shell with sliced fresh peaches, alternating with the glaze. Refrigerate.

It may be time to give your insurance an annual check-up. Locate your policies, have a specialist let you know if you have adequate coverage. Check homeowners coverage particularly if it would cost more to rebuild your house then when you bought.
Has your family grown? If so perhaps more life insurance would be appropriate.

The Financial Coaches' Chocolate Chip Cookies

Ingredients and Measurements:

1 cup butter, softened
1 cup packed brown sugar
2 teaspoons vanilla extracts
1 teaspoon baking soda
1/2 teaspoon salt
1 cup white sugar
2 eggs
3 cups all-purpose flour
2 teaspoons hot water
2 cups semisweet chocolate chips

Cooking Directions:

Preheat oven to 350 degrees
Cream together the butter, white sugar, and brown sugar until smooth. Beat in the eggs one at a time, then stir in the vanilla. Dissolve baking soda in hot water. Add to batter along with salt. Stir in flour, chocolate chips. Drop by large spoonful's onto ungreased pans; bake for about 10 minutes in the preheated oven, or until edges are nicely browned.

Here are some strategies for saving money. Dine in, not out. Reduce your cable channels or get rid of it completely, car pool or take rapid transit, give up a vice, (i.e. Alcohol), Grocery shop smarter, follow the advice in this book.

The Financial Coaches' Peanut without the Jelly Cookies

Ingredients and Measurements:

1 cup shortening
1 cup white sugar
1 cup packed brown sugar
1 cup peanut butter
2 eggs
2 tablespoons water
2 1/2 cups sifted all-purpose flour
1 teaspoon baking soda
1 teaspoon salt

Cooking Directions:

Preheat oven to 375 degrees. Beat the shortening with the sugars and the peanut butter until well mixed. Beat in the egg and the water. Gradually beat in the flour, baking soda and salt. Form cookies on an ungreased baking sheet with a cookie press or roll into balls and smash flat with a floured fork or fingers. Bake at 375 degrees for 12 minutes or more until done, usually when the puffed up cookie has lowered down to level; before then it is chewier.

When used car shopping, see if you can locate an individual dealer who is reputable, and will take you to a car auction. Usually, these people will work for a single fee, like $350.00 for the entire transaction. You are buying wholesale, and you don't have to work with a car dealership.

.

The Financial Coaches Long and Winding Rocky Road Cookies

Ingredients and Measurements:

1/2 cup butter
1 cup white sugar
1/2 teaspoon vanilla extracts
1/2 teaspoon baking powder
1 cup chopped walnuts
1 cup semisweet chocolate chips
2 eggs
1 1/2 cups all-purpose flour
1/4 teaspoon salt
48 miniature marshmallows

Cooking Directions:

Preheat oven to 400 degrees F (200 degrees C). In a small sauce melt together the butter and 1/2 cup of the chocolate chips, stirring frequently. Remove from heat and set aside to cool. In a medium bowl, stir together the melted chocolate mixture with the sugar, eggs and vanilla. Sift together the flour, baking powder and salt, stir into the chocolate mixture. Finally, stir in the chopped nuts and remaining chocolate chips. Drop dough by rounded teaspoonful's onto unprepared cookie sheets. Press a miniature marshmallow into the center of each cookie. Bake for 7 to 8 minutes in the preheated oven. Remove from baking sheets immediately to cool on wire racks.

Often times when cooking you have more than enough ingredients when making a casserole. Please don't ever throughout the excess ingredients. Either freeze it, or make a second smaller casserole, and freeze that.

Financial Coaches' "Hogan's Heroes" German Chocolate Cake

Ingredients and Measurements:

1/2 cup(s) boiling water
2 cup(s) all-purpose flour
1 teaspoon(s) baking soda
2 cup(s) sugar
4 large eggs, separated
1 cup(s) buttermilk
4 ounce(s) German's Chocolate, coarsely chopped
1/4 cup(s) cocoa
1 teaspoon(s) salt
1 cup(s) (2 sticks) unsalted butter, softened
1 teaspoon(s) vanilla

Cooking Direction:

Make batter: Preheat oven to 350 degrees F. Using a small brush, lightly coat two 9-inch cake pans with softened butter or vegetable-oil cooking spray. Dust with flour and tap out any excess. Set aside. In a medium heat-proof bowl, pour boiling water over German's Chocolate. Stir until smooth and set aside. In another medium bowl, combine flour, cocoa, baking soda, and salt. Set aside. In a large bowl, using a mixer set on medium-high speed, beat sugar and butter until very light, 1 to 2 minutes. Add egg yolks, one at a time, until well incorporated. Reduce mixer speed to low and add chocolate mixture and vanilla. Add flour mixture by thirds, alternating with buttermilk and ending with dry ingredients. Thoroughly clean mixer beaters. In a medium bowl, beat egg whites to soft peaks. Use a rubber spatula to gently stir half cup beaten whites into batter. Fold remaining whites into batter.
Bake cake: Divide batter equally between pans and spread evenly. Bake on middle rack of oven until a tester inserted in center of each cake layer comes out clean, 30 to 35 minutes. Cool in pans on a wire rack for 15 minutes. Use a knife to loosen cake from sides of pan and invert onto wire rack to cool completely.
Finish cake: Place 1 layer on a cake plate and top with 1/3 of our **Coconut-Pecan Filling**. Repeat with second and third layers and remaining filling. Serve or store in an airtight container at room temperature.

Since we are talking Germany, lower your travel expenses by; Buying tickets early and on Kayak.com. Pack light, do you really need 5 pairs of jeans. Stay at 3 star hotels instead of 4 stars, particularly if all you are doing is sleeping there. Never take a cruise, and use their excursion experts. Get off the boat, bargain yourself. Nothing is more fun to go snorkeling right next to your shipmates and paying 75% less, (except when you tell them).

The Financial Coaches" She Wore Red Velvet" Cake

Ingredients and Measurements:

1/2 cup(s) unsalted butter, softened
4 large egg yolks
1 1/2 teaspoon(s) vanilla extract
1 teaspoon(s) salt
2 1/4 cup(s) sifted cake flour
1 teaspoon(s) white vinegar

1 1/2 cup(s) sugar
3 tablespoon(s) red food coloring
1/4 cup(s) cocoa
1 cup(s) buttermilk
Teaspoon baking soda
Cooked Vanilla Icing

Cooking Direction:

Make batter: Preheat oven to 350 degrees F. Using a small brush, lightly coat two 9-inch cake pans with softened butter or vegetable-oil cooking spray. Dust with flour and tap out any excess. Set aside. In a medium heat-proof bowl, pour boiling water over German's Chocolate. Stir until smooth and set aside. In another medium bowl, combine flour, cocoa, baking soda, and salt. Set aside. In a large bowl, using a mixer set on medium-high speed, beat sugar and butter until very light, 1 to 2 minutes. Add egg yolks, one at a time, until well incorporated. Reduce mixer speed to low and add chocolate mixture and vanilla. Add flour mixture by thirds, alternating with buttermilk and ending with dry ingredients. Thoroughly clean mixer beaters. In a medium bowl, beat egg whites to soft peaks. Use a rubber spatula to gently stir half cup beaten whites into batter. Fold remaining whites into batter.
Bake cake: Divide batter equally between pans and spread evenly. Bake on middle rack of oven until a tester inserted in center of each cake layer comes out clean, 30 to 35 minutes. Cool in pans on a wire rack for 15 minutes. Use a knife to loosen cake from sides of pan and invert onto wire rack to cool completely.
Finish cake: Place 1 layer on a cake plate and top with 1/3 of our **Coconut-Pecan Filling**. Repeat with second and third layers and remaining filling. Serve or store in an airtight container at room temperature.

Inflate your car tires to tire company's recommendation, clean your air filter, use regular unleaded not super premium. This will save you a large percentage of money you are currently spending by not doing them.

The Financial Coaches' Chocolate Cream Pie

Ingredients and Measurements:

1 (9 inch) pie crust, baked
1 1/2 cups white sugar
1/2 cup unsweetened cocoa powder
3 cups milk 1 tablespoon butter
1 cup frozen whipped topping, thawed
3 egg yolks, beaten
3 tablespoons cornstarch
1/2 teaspoon salt
1 1/2 teaspoons vanilla extract

Cooking Directions:

In a large mixing bowl, cream together egg yolks and sugar; mix in cornstarch, cocoa powder, and salt. Add milk and stir gently. Pour mixture into a large saucepan and cook over medium heat, stirring constantly, until boiling. Remove from heat. Stir in butter or margarine and vanilla extract. Cool slightly, and then pour mixture into pastry shell. Chill before serving. Garnish with whipped topping.

The biggest problem with individuals seeking my help is that the individuals sometimes suffer from a disorder known as paralysis by analysis. Make a decision to save and stick with it.

Epilogue

The only cooking show I watch is Rachael Ray. I know what you are thinking. She is beautiful, sexy, bubbly, cute, did I say beautiful. She is also smart, a great cook, fun to watch, did I say sexy? I know; she very married. "Just because you are on a diet, does not mean you can't read the menu". I am obsessed...I use her cookware, kitchen tools; just about anything that has her picture on it. What I really admired is her ability to take a recipe and bring it to a level that the rest of us can understand. Let me make this clear. I am not a chef; I have no formal education in the culinary arts. What I do like is eating and tasting new foods. I find cooking to be fun and relaxing. However, when someone tastes my meals, and you see a look of happiness and contentment on their face, that coupled with meals that are affordable for most people, it simply is a great feeling.

I feel the last word on "Coupon Warriors" in this book should come from a young lady who has been a guest on my radio show. Her name is Donna Styron. She is a true coupon warrior. She started her interview with the following; the question I asked was," why do you coupon"?

To save money of course, Oh and it is the best adrenaline rush. To be able to walk out of that store knowing you saved yourself a ton of money, who wouldn't like that feeling?"

I couldn't have said it better myself.

DAK

www.ingramcontent.com/pod-product-compliance
Ingram Content Group UK Ltd.
Pitfield, Milton Keynes, MK11 3LW, UK
UKHW051136260726
13967UKWH00010B/3076